UKULELE

GOLD

GREATEST HITS

ISBN 978-1-5400-1213-5

HAL•LEONARD®

7777 W. BLUEMOUND RD. P.O. BOX 13819 MILWAUKEE, WI 53213

In Australia Contact:
Hal Leonard Australia Pty. Ltd.
4 Lentara Court
Cheltenham, Victoria, 3192 Australia
Email: ausadmin@halleonard.com.au

Visit Hal Leonard Online at
www.halleonard.com

CONTENTS

Chiquitita

Words and Music by Benny Andersson and Björn Ulvaeus

there is no way   you can   de - ny   it. _____
now   I   see   you've   bro - ken   a   feath - er. _____
there is no way   you can   de - ny   it. _____

I _____   can   see   that you're,   oh,   so   sad,   so   qui - et. ____
I _____   hope   we can patch   it   up   to - geth - er. ___
I _____   see   that you're,   oh,   so   sad,   so   qui - et. ____

1.
2. Chi - qui - ti - ta,   tell   me   the

2., 3.
Chi - qui - ti - ta,   you   and   I ____

Chorus

know   how   the   heart - aches come and they go and the   scars they're leav - in'. ___

You'll be   danc - in'   once a - gain, ___   and the   pain   will   end.   You will have   no

time   for   griev - in'. ___   Chi - qui - ti - ta,   you   and   I ___   cry,

Does Your Mother Know

Words and Music by Benny Andersson and Björn Ulvaeus

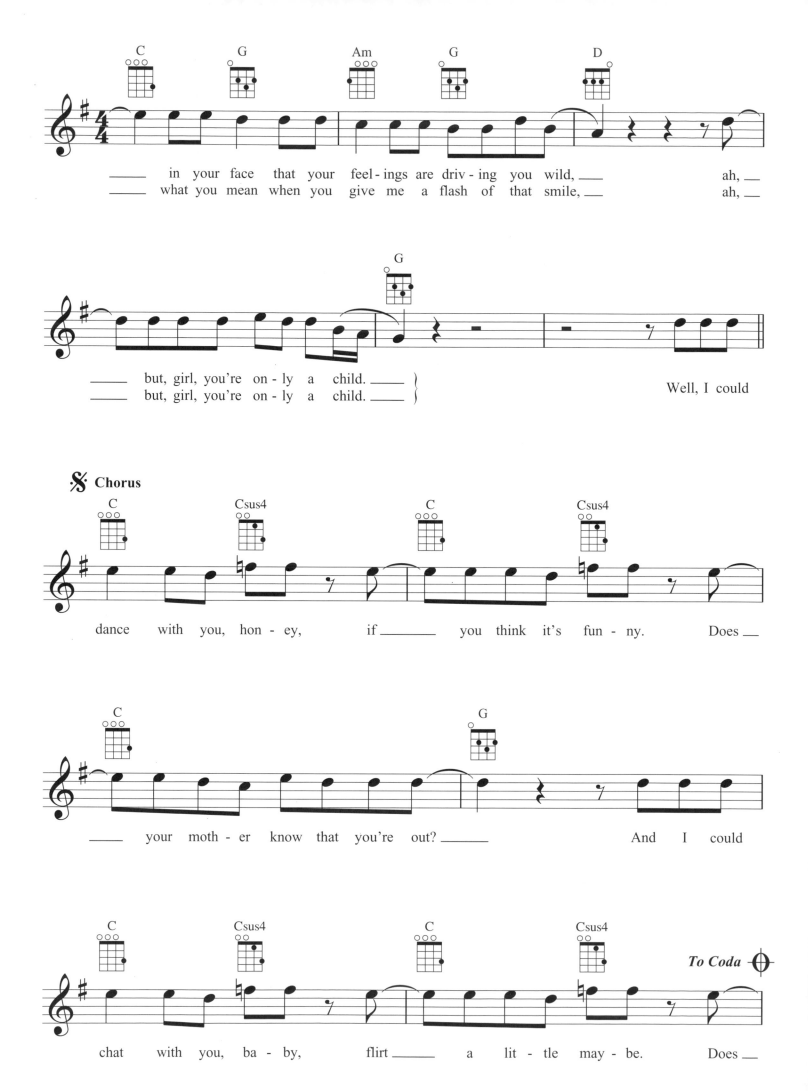

in your face that your feel - ings are driv - ing you wild, ___ ah, ___
what you mean when you give me a flash of that smile, ___ ah, ___

but, girl, you're on - ly a child. _____
but, girl, you're on - ly a child. _____

Well, I could

Chorus

dance with you, hon - ey, if _____ you think it's fun - ny. Does ___

your moth - er know that you're out? _____ And I could

chat with you, ba - by, flirt _____ a lit - tle may - be. Does ___

8

your moth-er know that you're out? ____ Take it eas - y, (take it eas - y,) bet - ter

slow down, girl. ____ That's no way to go. ____ (Does your moth - er know?) ____ Take it

eas - y, (take it eas - y,) try to cool it, girl. ____ Play it nice and slow. ___ (Does your

1.
moth - er know?) ___

2.
moth - er know?) ___
D.S. al Coda
Well, I could

Coda

your moth - er know that you're out? _____

Dancing Queen

Words and Music by Benny Andersson, Björn Ulvaeus and Stig Anderson

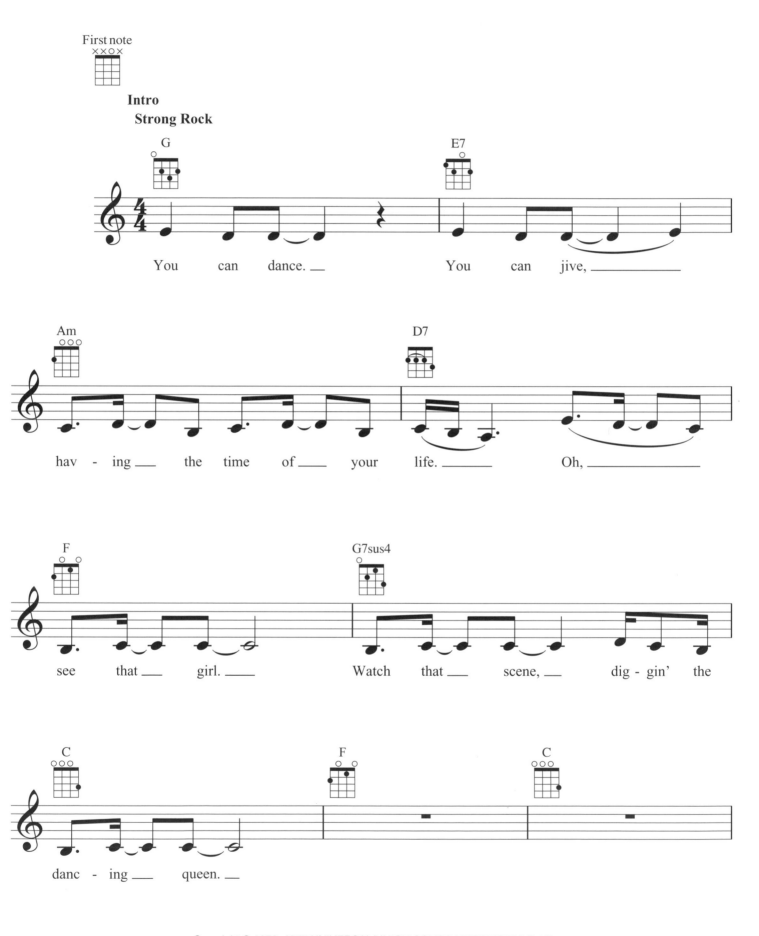

high.
gone,

With a bit ____ of rock mu - sic,
look - ing out ____ for an - oth - er.

ev - 'ry - thing ____ is fine.
An - y - one ____ will do.

You're in the mood for a dance, ____

and when ____ you get the ____ chance, ____

Chorus

____ you are ____ the danc - ing ____ queen, ____ young and ____ sweet, ____ on - ly

sev - en - teen. ____

Danc - ing ____ queen, ____

feel the ____ beat ____ from the tam - bou - rine. ____

You can dance. __ You can jive, ____

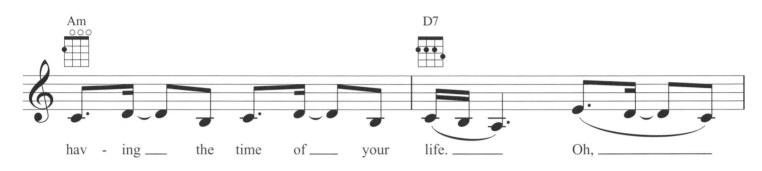

hav - ing ___ the time of ___ your life. ____ Oh, _____

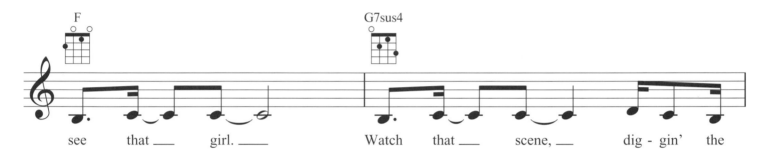

see that ___ girl. ____ Watch that ___ scene, ___ dig - gin' the

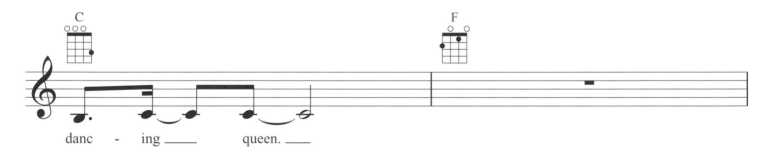

danc - ing ____ queen. ____

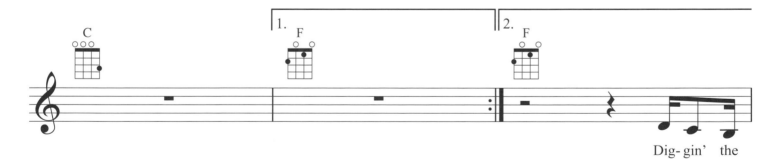

Dig- gin' the

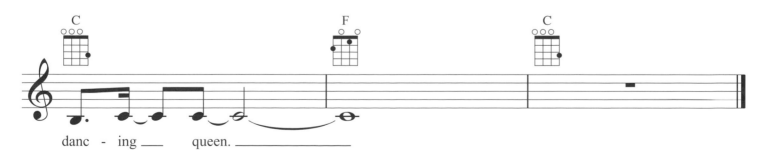

danc - ing ___ queen. _____

Fernando

Words and Music by Benny Andersson, Björn Ulvaeus and Stig Anderson

1. Can you hear the drums, Fer - nan - do?
2. They were clos - er now, Fer - nan - do.
3. Now we're old and grey, Fer - nan - do,

I re - mem - ber long a - go an - oth - er star - ry night like
Ev - 'ry ho - ur, ev - 'ry min - ute seemed to last e - ter - nal -
and since man - y years I have - n't seen a ri - fle in your

this.
ly.
hand.

In the fi - re - light, Fer - nan - do,
I was so a - fraid, Fer - nan - do,
Can you hear the drums, Fer - nan - do?

you were hum - ming to your - self and soft - ly strum - ming your gui -
we were young and full of life and none of us pre - pared to
Do you still re - call the fright - ful night we crossed the Ri - o

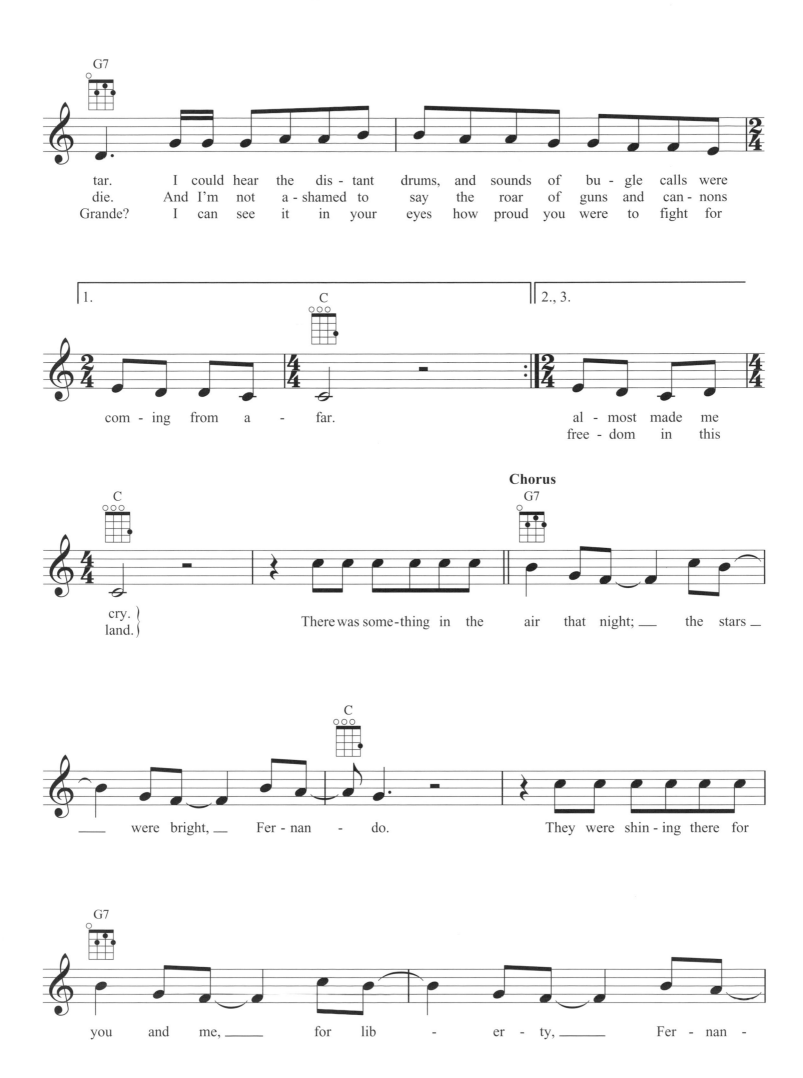

tar.   I could hear the dis - tant drums, and sounds of bu - gle calls were
die.   And I'm not a - shamed to say the roar of guns and can - nons
Grande?   I can see it in your eyes how proud you were to fight for

1.

com - ing from a - far.

2., 3.

al - most made me
free - dom in this

cry.
land.

Chorus

There was some-thing in the air that night; ___ the stars ___

___ were bright, ___ Fer - nan - do.

They were shin - ing there for

you and me, ___ for lib - er - ty, ___ Fer - nan -

15

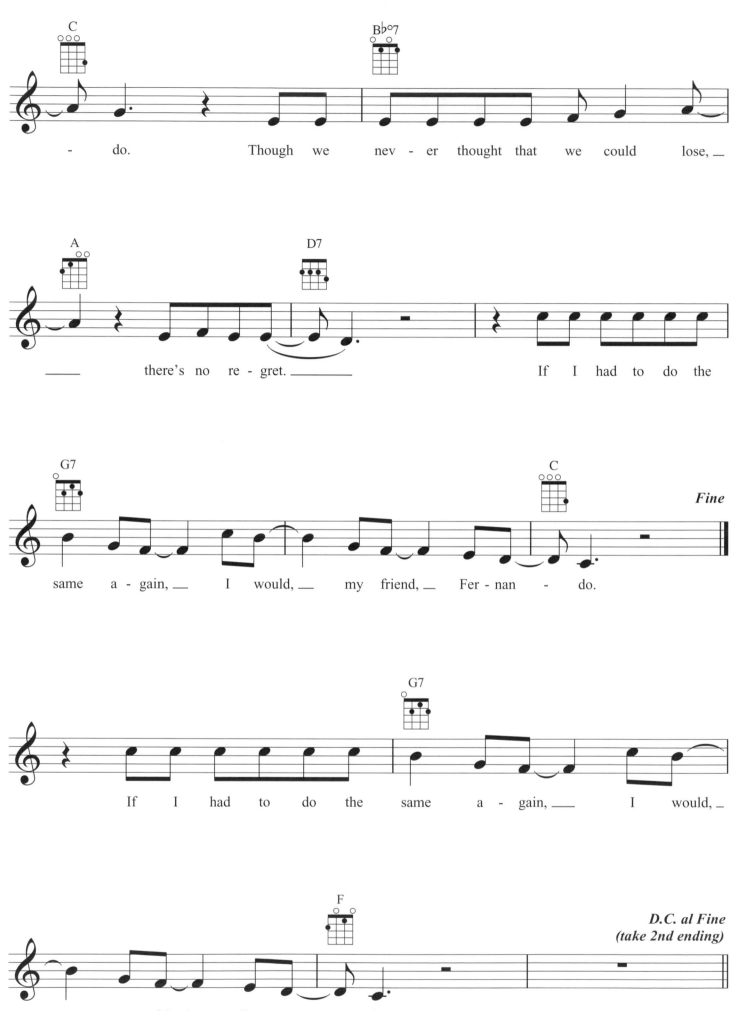

Gimme! Gimme! Gimme!
(A Man After Midnight)

Words and Music by Benny Andersson and Björn Ulvaeus

1. Half past twelve, and I'm watch-in' the late ___ show in my
2. Mov - ie stars find the end of the rain - bow with a

flat all a - lone. ___ How I hate to spend the eve - ning on my
for - tune to win. ___ It's so dif - f'rent from the world ___ I'm liv - in'

own. Au - tumn winds blow-in' out - side my win - dow as I
in. Tired of T - V, I o - pen the win - dow, and I

look a - round the room ___ and it makes me so de - pressed ___ to see the
gaze in - to the night, ___ but there's noth - ing there to see, ___ no one in

gloom.
sight.

There's not a soul out there, ___

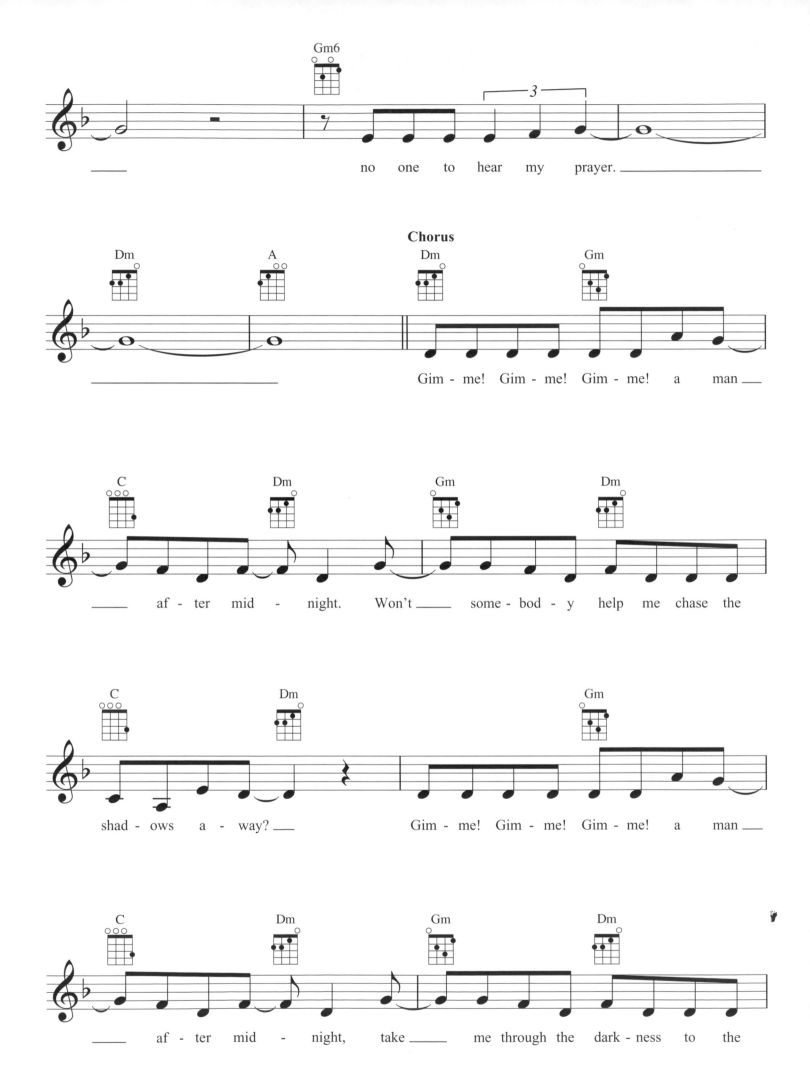

I Have a Dream

Words and Music by Benny Andersson and Björn Ulvaeus

Chorus

fail.
mile.

I be - lieve in an - gels, some - thing good in ev - 'ry - thing I see. I be - lieve in an - gels when I know the time is right for me. I'll cross the stream, I have a dream.

1. 2. I have a

2. I'll cross the

stream, I have a dream.

Knowing Me, Knowing You

Words and Music by Benny Andersson, Björn Ulvaeus and Stig Anderson

1. No more care-free laugh-ter,
2. Mem - 'ries, good days, bad days,

si - lence ev - er
they'll be with me

af - ter.
al - ways.

Walk - ing through an emp - ty house,
In these old fa - mil - iar rooms

tears in my eyes.
chil - dren would play.

This is where the sto - ry ends, this is good-bye.
Now there's on - ly emp - ti - ness, noth-ing to say.

Chorus

Know-ing me, know-ing you, there is noth-ing we can do. ___

___ Know-ing me, know-ing you, we just have to face it, this time ___

___ we're through. Break-in' up is nev-er

eas-y, I know, but I have to go. Know-ing

me, know-ing you, ___ it's the best _____ I can do.

do.

Mamma Mia

Words and Music by Benny Andersson, Björn Ulvaeus and Stig Anderson

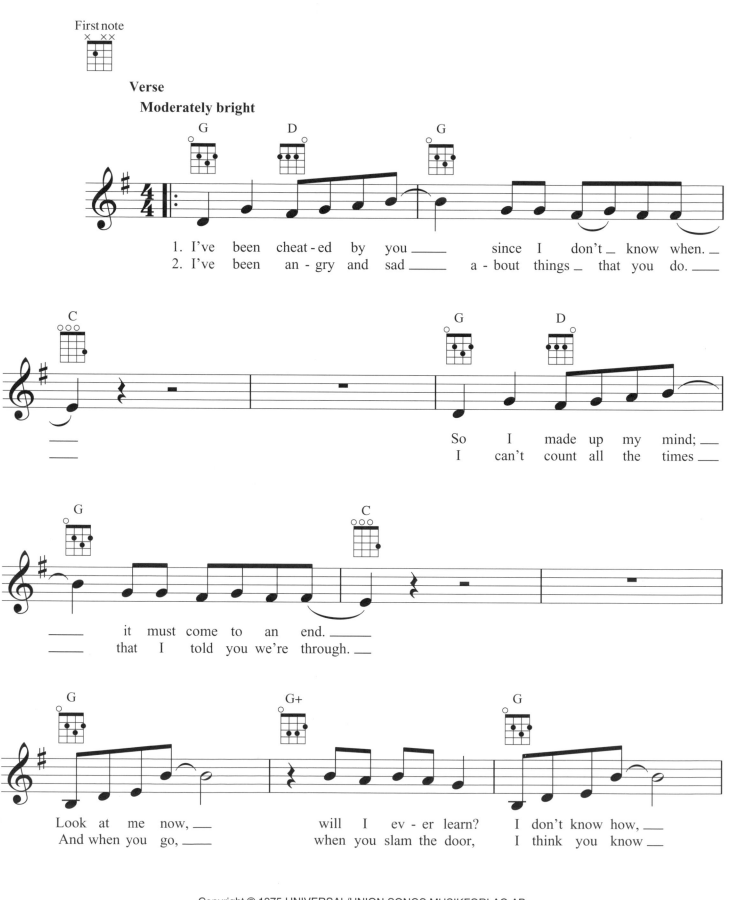

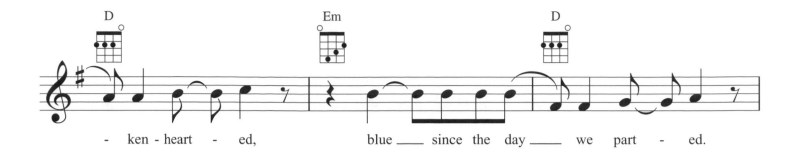

- ken - heart - ed, blue ___ since the day ___ we part - ed.

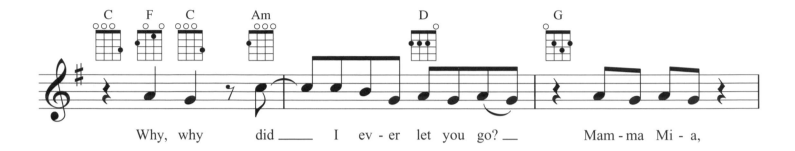

Why, why did ___ I ev - er let you go? ___ Mam - ma Mi - a,

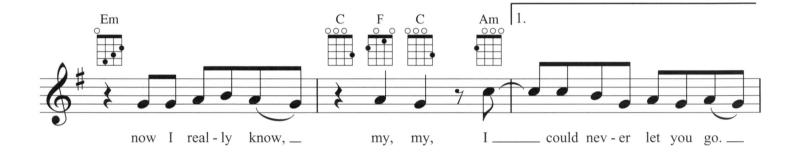

now I real - ly know, ___ my, my, I ___ could nev - er let you go. ___

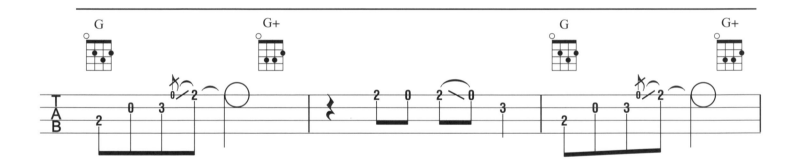

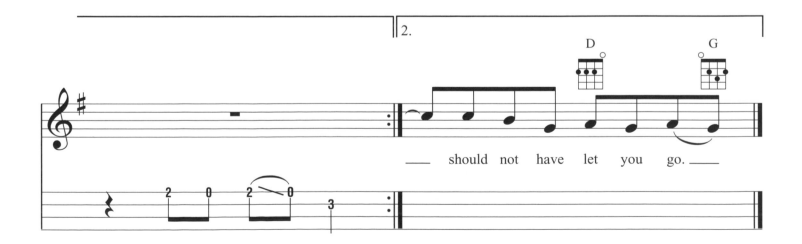

___ should not have let you go. ___

Lay All Your Love on Me

Words and Music by Benny Andersson and Björn Ulvaeus

Money, Money, Money

Words and Music by Benny Andersson and Björn Ulvaeus

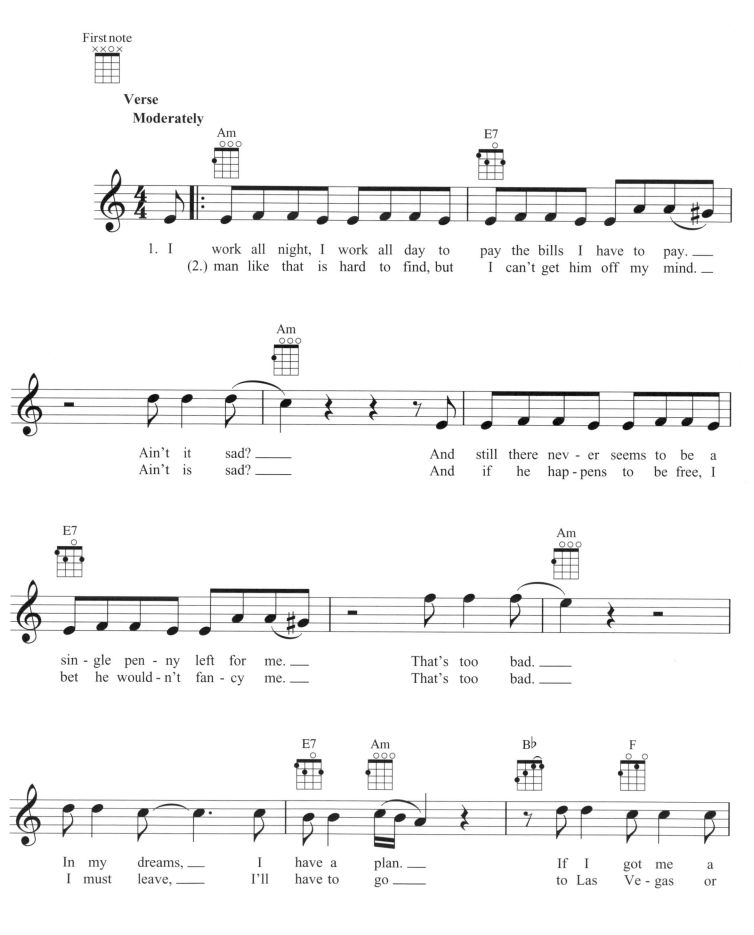

wealth - y man, _____   I would - n't have to work at all; I'd
Mon - a - co, _____   and win a for - tune in a game. My

fool a - round and have a ball. _____)
life would nev - er be the same. _____)

Chorus

Mon - ey, mon - ey, mon - ey   must be fun - ny   in a rich man's world. _

_____   Mon - ey, mon - ey, mon - ey,   al - ways sun - ny

in a rich man's world. _____   A - ha, _____

Bridge

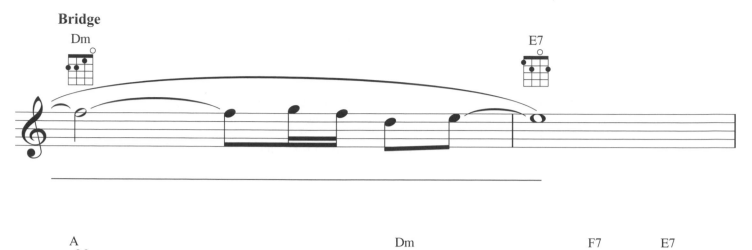

all   the   things   I   could   do _____   if   I

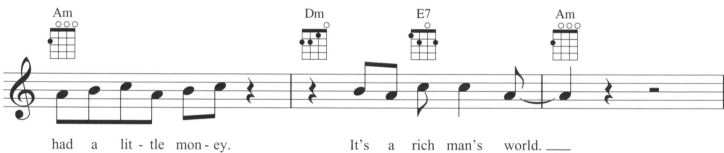

had   a   lit - tle   mon - ey.   It's   a   rich   man's   world. ____

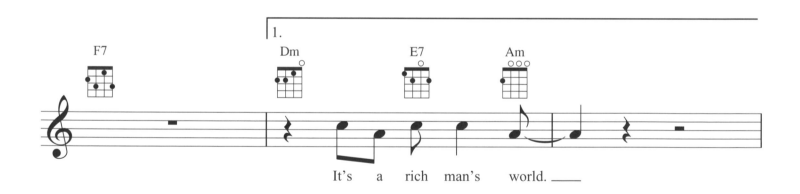

1.

It's   a   rich   man's   world. ____

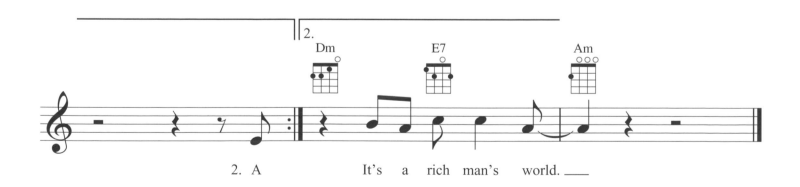

2.

2. A   It's   a   rich   man's   world. ____

Super Trouper

Words and Music by Benny Andersson and Björn Ulvaeus

1. I was sick and tired of ev-'ry-thing when I called ___ you last night from
2. Fac-ing twen-ty thou-sand of your friends, how can an - y-one be so

Glas - gow. All I do is eat and sleep and sing, wish-ing ev-
lone - ly? Part of a suc-cess that nev-er ends, still I'm think-

- 'ry show was the last ___ show. So i-mag-ine I was
- ing a-bout you on - ly. There are mo-ments when I

glad to hear you're com-ing; sud-den-ly I feel al - right.
think I'm go-ing cra-zy, but it's gon-na be al - right.

And it's gon - na be so dif - f'rent when I'm on the stage to - night. _____

Ev - 'ry - thing will be so dif - f'rent when I'm on the stage to - night. _____

%. Chorus

_____ } To - night the su - per trou - per lights are gon - na find _ me,

shin - ing like the sun, smil - ing, hav - ing

fun, feel - ing like a num - ber one. To - night the

su - per trou - per beams are gon - na blind _ me, but I won't feel

blue like I al - ways do, 'cause

To Coda

34

some - where   in   the   crowd ___ there's   you.

some -where   in   the   crowd _ there's   you.   So   I'll   be

Bridge

there   when   you   ar - rive;   the   sight   of   you   will   prove   to   me   I'm   still   a -

live. And   when   you   take   me   in   your   arms   and   hold   me   tight,   I

D.S. al Coda

know   it's   gon - na   mean   so   much   to - night. _____   To - night   the

Coda

some - where   in   the   crowd ___ there's   you.

The Name of the Game

Words and Music by Benny Andersson, Björn Ulvaeus and Stig Anderson

Em   Fmaj7 5fr   Am

no one ev - er could   reach _____ me.   But I think I can
and the way you see   through ___ me,   got a feel - ing you

D   Em   Fmaj7 5fr

see in your face   there's a lot you can   teach _____ me. _____
gim - me no choice,   but it means a lot   to _____ me. _____

Dm7   G7sus4

___ } So I wan - na know,   what's the name of the game? _

Chorus

C   Fmaj7 5fr   G   G7

___   Does it mean an - y - thing _____ to you? _

C   F   G   F

___   What's the name of the game? _

C   F   G   G7

_____   Can you feel it the way _____ I do? _

Tell me, please, ___ 'cuz I have to know. ___

___ I'm a bash-ful child ___ be-gin-ning to grow. ___

___ And you make me talk, ___ and you

make me feel, ___ and you make me show ___

___ what I'm try-ing to ___ con-ceal. If I trust in you, ___

___ would you let me down, ___ would you

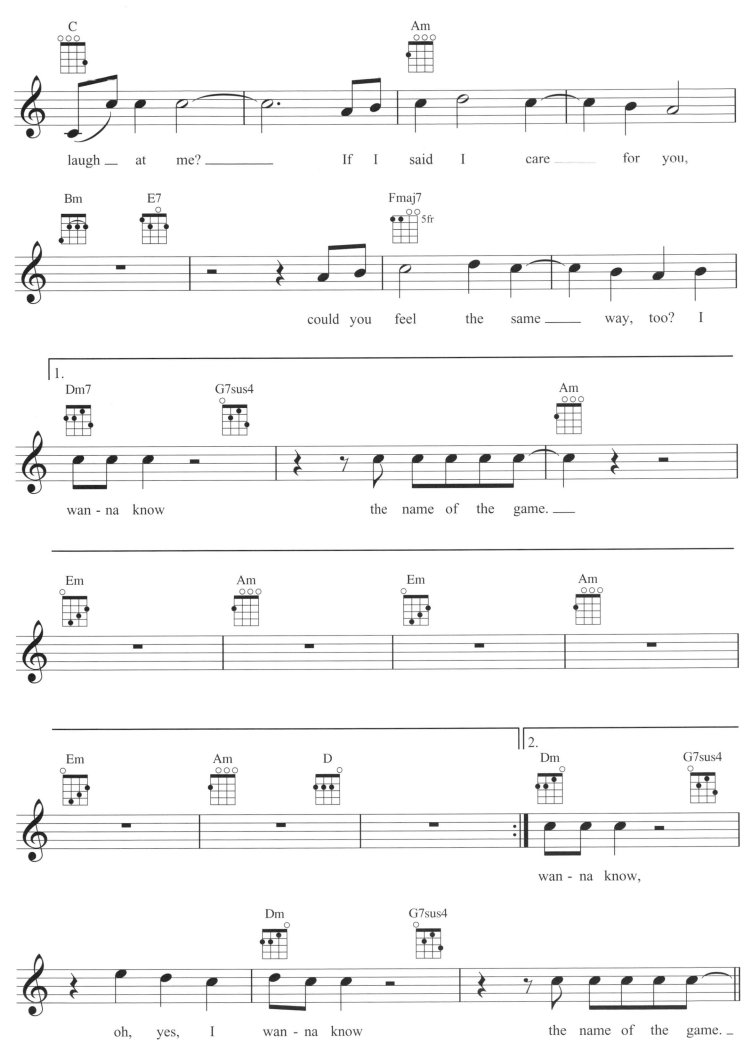

laugh __ at me? _____ If I said I care _____ for you,

could you feel the same _____ way, too? I

1.
wan - na know the name of the game. ____

2.
wan - na know,

oh, yes, I wan - na know the name of the game. __

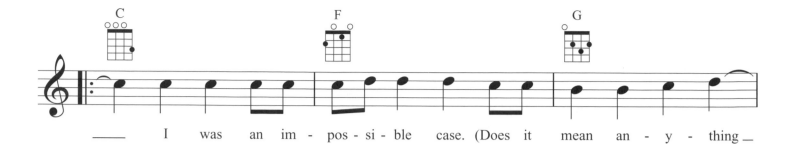

_____ I was an im - pos - si - ble case. (Does it mean an - y - thing _

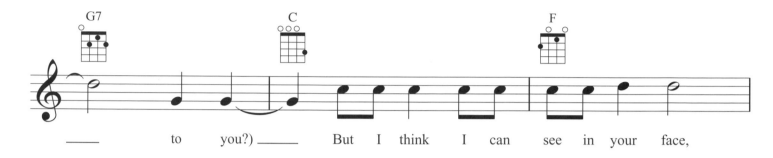

_____ to you?) _____ But I think I can see in your face,

and it means that I _____ love _____ you. (What's the name of the game?) _

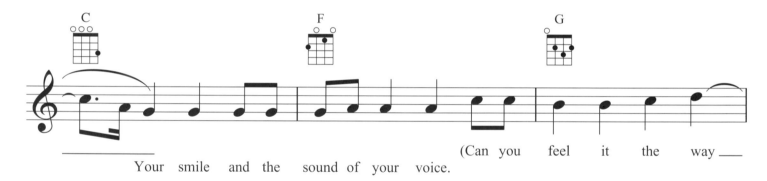

_____ (Can you feel it the way _

Your smile and the sound of your voice.

_____ I do?) _____ Got a feel - ing you give me no choice,

Repeat and fade

but it means that I _____ love _____ you. (What's the name of the game?) _

Thank You for the Music

Words and Music by Benny Andersson and Björn Ulvaeus

grate - ful and proud; ___ all I want ___
mel - o - dy can? ____ Well, who - ev -

___ is to sing ___ it out loud. _____ } So I say
- er it was, ___ I'm a fan. _____ }

𝄋 Chorus

(1., 2.) thank you for the mu - sic, the songs I'm sing - ing; }
(D.S.) Thank you for the mu - sic, the songs I'm sing - ing; }

thanks for all the joy they're bring - ing. Who can live with - out it? I

ask in all hon - es - ty. _____ What would life be? ___

___ With - out a song ___ or dance, __ what are we? So I say

One of Us

Words and Music by Benny Andersson and Björn Ulvaeus

Waterloo

Words and Music by Benny Andersson, Björn Ulvaeus and Stig Anderson

Chorus

- ter - loo, I _____ was de - feat - ed; you won ___ the war.

Wa - ter - loo, prom - ise to love ___ you for - ev -

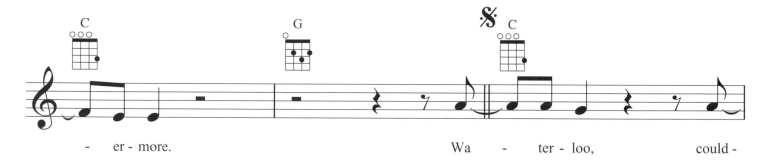

- er - more. Wa - ter - loo, could -

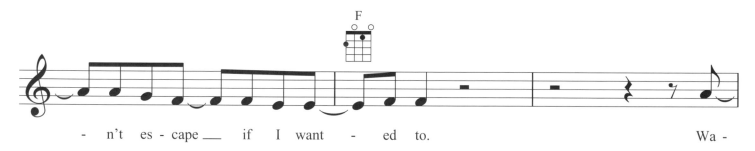

- n't es - cape ___ if I want - ed to. Wa -

- ter - loo, know - ing my fate ___ is to be ___ with you. Wa -

To Coda

- Wa - Wa - Wa - Wa - ter - loo, fi - nal - ly fac - ing my Wa -

S.O.S.

Words and Music by Benny Andersson, Björn Ulvaeus and Stig Anderson

First note

Verse
Strong Rock tempo

1. Where are those hap - py days? __ They seem so hard __ to find. __
2. You seem so far a - way __ though you are stand - ing near. __

__ I try to reach __ for you, __
__ You made me feel __ a - live, __

__ but you have closed __ your mind.
__ but some - thing died, __ I fear.

Pre-Chorus

What - ev - er hap - pened to _____ our love?
I real - ly tried to make _____ it out.

I wish I un - der - stood. _____
I wish I un - der - stood. _____

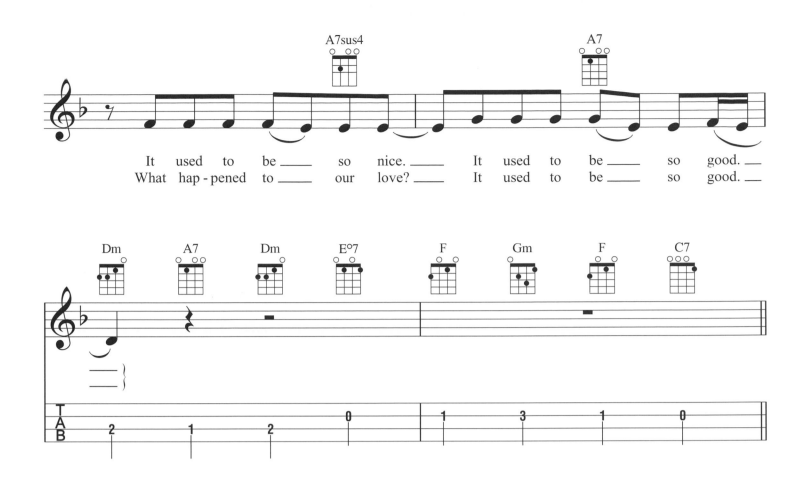

It used to be ____ so nice. ____ It used to be ____ so good. ____
What hap-pened to ____ our love? ____ It used to be ____ so good. ____

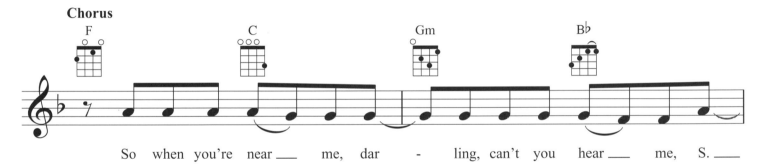

Chorus

So when you're near ____ me, dar - ling, can't you hear ____ me, S. ____

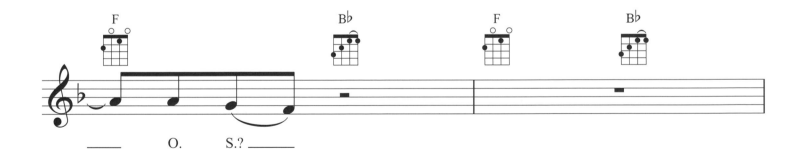

____ O. S.? ____

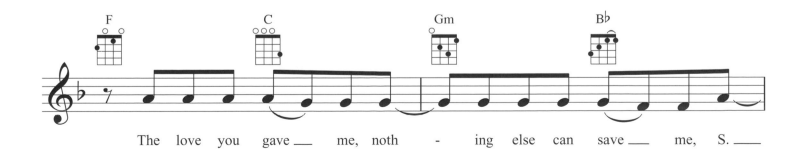

The love you gave ____ me, noth - ing else can save ____ me, S. ____

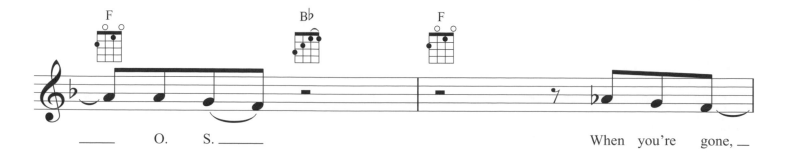

_____ O. S. _____   When you're gone, __

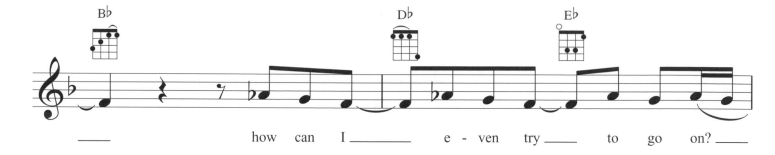

__   how can I _____ e - ven try _____ to go on? _____

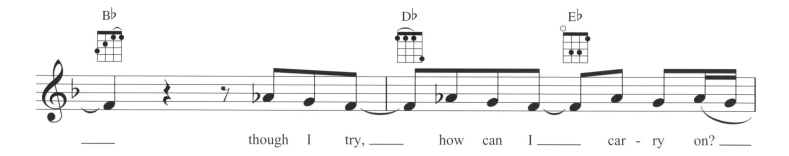

__   When you're gone, __

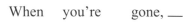

__   though I try, _____ how can I _____ car - ry on? _____

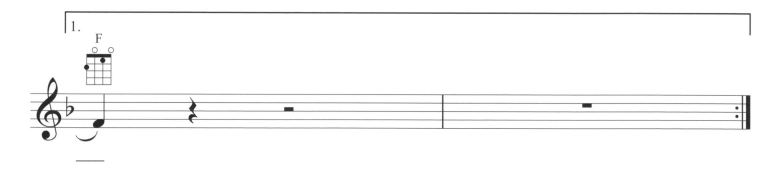

__

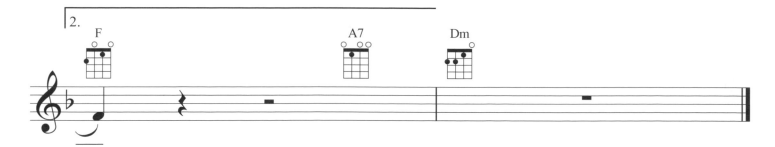

The Winner Takes It All

Words and Music by Benny Andersson and Björn Ulvaeus

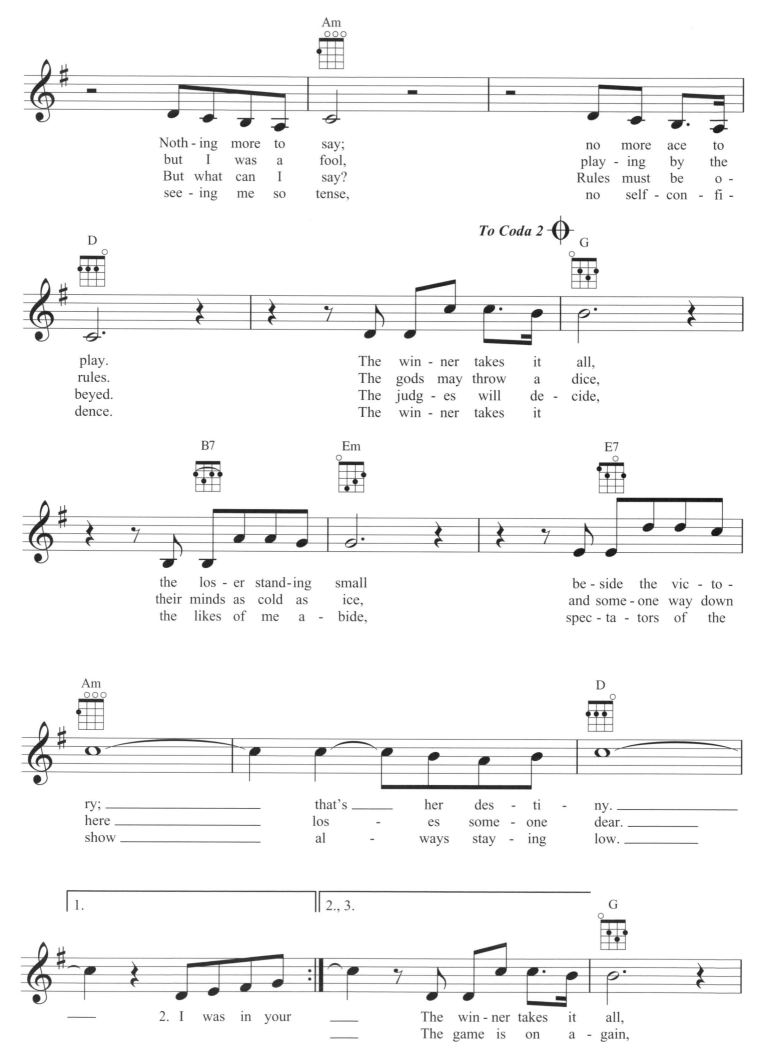

To Coda 2

Noth - ing more to say;		no more ace to	play.
but I was a fool,		play - ing by the	rules.
But what can I say?		Rules must be o -	beyed.
see - ing me so tense,		no self - con - fi -	dence.

The win - ner takes it all,	the los - er stand-ing small	be - side the vic - to - ry; _____
The gods may throw a dice,	their minds as cold as ice,	and some - one way down here _____
The judg - es will de - cide,	the likes of me a - bide,	spec - ta - tors of the show _____
The win - ner takes it		

that's _____ her des - ti - ny. _____	
los - es some - one dear. _____	
al - ways stay - ing low. _____	

1.
_____
2. I was in your _____

2., 3.
The win - ner takes it all,
The game is on a - gain,

Take a Chance on Me

Words and Music by Benny Andersson and Björn Ulvaeus

- y best, and it ain't no lie. _____ If you put me to _____ the test, if you

C   Dm   G

let me try, _____ take a chance on me, _____ take a

Dm   G   **Verse** Dm

chance on me. _____   1. We can go _____ danc - ing,
                                  2. Oh, you can take your time, _ ba - by,

C

we can go _____ walk - ing, _____ as long as we're _ to - geth - er.
I'm in no _____ hur - ry; _____ I know I'm gon - na get _____ you.

Dm

Lis - ten to _____ some mu - sic,   may - be just _ talk - ing, _ you'd
You don't wan - na hurt _ me,   ba - by, don't _ wor - ry; _____

C

get to know _ me bet - ter.   'Cause you know I got
I ain't gon - na let _____ you.   Let me tell you now.

me know; gon-na be a - round. _____ If you got no place _____

_____ to go when you're feel-ing down. _____ If you're all a - lone _____

_____ when the pret - ty birds _____ have flown, hon - ey, I'm still free; _____

_____ take a chance on me. _____ Gon-na do my ver -

- y best, ba - by, can't you see. _____ Got - ta put me to _____

Repeat and Fade

_____ the test; take a chance on me. _____ If you change your mind, _____

Voulez-Vous

Words and Music by Benny Andersson and Björn Ulvaeus

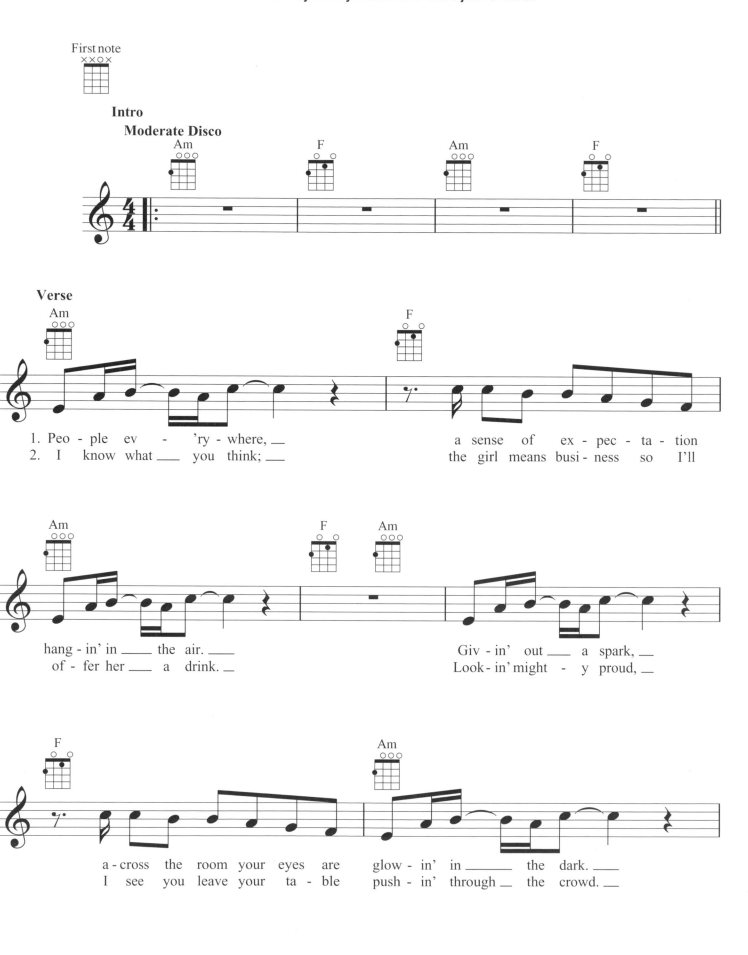